The Unforgiving Heart

SHAWN FELTON

Published by SHAWN FELTON, 2024.

THE UNFORGIVING HEART

First edition. June 12, 2024.

Copyright © 2024 SHAWN FELTON.

ISBN: 979-8227682215

Written by SHAWN FELTON.

Table of Contents

BIblical Perspectives on Forgiveness : The Unforgiving Heart

Introduction

In a world often marred by conflict, bitterness, and division, the concept of forgiveness stands as a beacon of hope and healing. Forgiveness is not only a central tenet of the Christian faith but also a universal human need that transcends religious boundaries. Contemporary society grapples with deep-seated wounds, both personal and societal, that cry out for the balm of forgiveness. This book seeks to explore the steadfast perspective of the human heart on forgiveness, drawing wisdom from the eternal truths of Scripture and the lived experiences of people throughout history.

The Bible offers a rich tapestry of teachings on forgiveness, woven through the narratives of patriarchs, kings, prophets, and ultimately, the life and teachings of Jesus Christ. From the Old Testament accounts of Joseph forgiving his brothers to the profound parables of Jesus on forgiveness, the Scriptures provide a profound well from which to draw insight and guidance.

This book aims to be a comprehensive guide to understanding forgiveness from a biblical perspective. It will delve into the critical aspects of forgiveness, exploring its definition, types, and the reasons why it can be so challenging to extend forgiveness to those who have wronged us. We will examine the consequences of unforgiveness and the transformative power that forgiveness can have in our lives, relationships, and communities.

Through a careful study of Scripture, this book will illuminate the imperative of absolute forgiveness in biblical terms, offering divine wisdom and practical tools for cultivating a forgiving heart. Relevant scripture verses will be woven throughout, providing a solid foundation for our exploration of this crucial topic.

Ultimately, this book is a clarion call for contemporary society to embrace forgiveness as a way of life, a path to healing and restoration. By understanding forgiveness from a biblical perspective, we can unlock its transformative potential and experience the freedom, peace, and joy that come from living a life centered on the radical love and forgiveness exemplified by Christ.

Part 1: Understanding Forgiveness
Chapter 1: What is Forgiveness?

Forgiveness is a concept that is often misunderstood or oversimplified. At its core, forgiveness is a conscious decision to let go of resentment, anger, and bitterness towards someone who has wronged us. It involves a deliberate choice to extend mercy, compassion, and grace to the offender, regardless of whether they have asked for or deserve it.

Forgiveness is not the same as pardoning, excusing, or reconciling. Pardoning involves absolving someone of the consequences of their actions, while excusing involves justifying or minimizing the offense. Reconciliation, on the other hand, is the restoration of a broken relationship, which may or may not follow forgiveness. Forgiveness, however, is an internal process that takes place within the heart of the one who has been wronged, regardless of the offender's response or actions.

It is important to note that forgiveness does not mean condoning or approving of the offense committed. It does not diminish the gravity of the wrongdoing or absolve the offender of responsibility. Rather, forgiveness is a conscious choice to release the offender from the debt they owe us, liberating us from the burden of carrying resentment and bitterness.

Furthermore, forgiveness can be classified into two main types: interpersonal forgiveness and divine forgiveness. Interpersonal forgiveness involves forgiving another person for a wrong they have committed against us, while divine forgiveness refers to our need for forgiveness from God for our sins and transgressions against Him.

In the Bible, we find numerous examples and teachings that illuminate the concept of forgiveness. One powerful illustration is found in the story of Joseph, who forgave his brothers for selling him into slavery (**Genesis 45:1-15**). Despite the depth of their betrayal, Joseph chose to extend forgiveness, recognizing that his suffering had ultimately been part of God's plan.

Jesus Christ, in his teachings and through his ultimate sacrifice on the cross, exemplified the highest form of forgiveness. In the Lord's Prayer, he instructed his followers to pray, "Forgive us our debts, as we also have forgiven our debtors" (**Matthew 6:12**), underscoring the fundamental link between receiving forgiveness from God and extending forgiveness to others.

As we delve deeper into the concept of forgiveness, it is crucial to understand that it is not a one-time event but rather a journey, a process that often requires intentional effort and perseverance. It is a decision that must be made repeatedly, as the wounds of the past can sometimes resurface, tempting us to hold onto bitterness and resentment.

Chapter 2: The Reasons Forgiveness is Difficult

While forgiveness is a noble and necessary pursuit, it is undeniably challenging for many people. The reasons why forgiveness can be so difficult are multifaceted and deeply rooted in our human experience.

One of the primary reasons forgiveness is challenging is the depth of the hurt or betrayal experienced. When we have been deeply wounded, whether physically, emotionally, or psychologically, the pain can be overwhelming, making it nearly impossible to extend forgiveness to the perpetrator. The greater the harm inflicted, the harder it can be to let go of the resentment and bitterness that accompany the injury.

Another reason forgiveness is difficult is the sense of injustice or violation of trust that often accompanies wrongdoing. When someone has breached our trust or violated our sense of fairness and justice, it can feel deeply personal and damaging. The need for accountability and consequences can make forgiveness feel like an act of minimizing or excusing the offense, even though true forgiveness does not negate the need for justice.

Pride and the desire for retribution can also hinder our ability to forgive. Human nature often craves revenge or a sense of repayment for the harm done to us. Letting go of that desire for retaliation or punishment can feel like a surrender or a failure to stand up for ourselves.

Additionally, forgiveness can be complicated by the fear of appearing weak or being taken advantage of again. There is a perception that forgiving someone who has wronged us makes us vulnerable to further hurt or exploitation, which can make forgiveness feel like a risky proposition.

In some cases, the difficulty in forgiveness stems from a lack of repentance or remorse from the offender. When the person who has wronged us shows no contrition or fails to acknowledge the harm they have caused, it can make forgiveness feel like a one-sided act of grace that may go unappreciated or unreciprocated.

Lastly, forgiveness can be challenging due to the deeply ingrained human tendency to hold onto grudges and perpetuate cycles of hurt and retaliation. Letting go of the desire for vengeance or recompense can be a countercultural act, requiring a conscious effort to break free from the patterns of bitterness and resentment that can become deeply rooted in our hearts and minds.

Despite these challenges, the Bible offers a clear call to forgiveness, recognizing both its difficulty and its profound importance. In **Matthew 18:21-22**, Jesus instructs his disciples to forgive "seventy times seven," emphasizing the limitless nature of forgiveness. The Apostle Paul echoes this sentiment, urging believers to "be kind to one another, tenderhearted, forgiving one another, as God in Christ forgave you" (**Ephesians 4:32**).

Chapter 3: The Consequences of Unforgiveness

While forgiveness is undoubtedly challenging, the consequences of unforgiveness can be devastating, both on a personal and societal level. Unforgiveness is a poison that corrodes the human soul, hindering our ability to experience true freedom, peace, and joy.

On a personal level, unforgiveness can lead to a host of negative emotional and psychological consequences. When we hold onto bitterness and resentment, it can breed anger, anxiety, depression, and even physical ailments. Unforgiveness is a heavy burden to bear, weighing us down with the baggage of past hurts and grievances.

Unforgiveness can also strain and damage our relationships with others. When we harbor resentment towards someone, it creates a barrier that hinders open communication, trust, and intimacy. Relationships become strained, and the potential for further conflict and misunderstanding increases.

In families and communities, unforgiveness can perpetuate cycles of hurt, retaliation, and division. Grudges and grievances can be passed down from generation to generation, creating a toxic environment of mistrust and enmity. This not only fractures relationships but can also undermine the fabric of society itself.

Furthermore, unforgiveness can hinder our spiritual growth and relationship with God. When we refuse to forgive others, we effectively close our hearts to the very forgiveness and grace that God has extended to us through Christ. This spiritual blockage can stunt our spiritual maturity and distance us from the transformative power of God's love and mercy.

The Bible offers numerous warnings about the dangers of unforgiveness. In **Matthew 6:15,** Jesus states, "But if you do not forgive others their trespasses, neither will your Father forgive.

Part 2: Forgiveness in the Bible
Chapter 1: Old Testament Teachings on Forgiveness

The theme of forgiveness is woven throughout the tapestry of the Old Testament, revealing the heart of God and His desire for reconciliation with His people. From the very beginning, when sin first entered the world, God extended the promise of redemption and forgiveness (**Genesis 3:15**). This set the stage for a narrative that would unfold over centuries, demonstrating God's steadfast love and mercy toward a people who repeatedly turned away from Him.

One of the most powerful examples of forgiveness in the Old Testament is found in the story of Joseph. After being betrayed and sold into slavery by his brothers, Joseph endured years of hardship and injustice. However, when he was eventually reunited with his brothers, he chose to extend forgiveness, declaring, "You meant evil against me, but God meant it for good" (**Genesis 50:20**). Joseph's ability to forgive his brothers for their grievous offense against him is a testament to the transformative power of forgiveness and the capacity for human beings to rise above bitterness and resentment.

The life of King David also provides a poignant illustration of the necessity of forgiveness and God's willingness to extend it. Despite his grievous sin with Bathsheba and the subsequent murder of her husband, Uriah, David was ultimately forgiven by God when he genuinely repented (**2 Samuel 12:13**). This act of divine forgiveness serves as a reminder that no sin is beyond the reach of God's mercy and that true repentance opens the door to forgiveness and restoration.

Throughout the Old Testament, the prophets consistently called upon the people of Israel to repent and turn back to God, promising forgiveness and restoration for those who did so. The prophet Isaiah declared, "Though your sins are like scarlet, they shall be as white as snow; though they are red as crimson, they shall become like wool" (**Isaiah 1:18**). This powerful imagery underscores the transformative power of God's forgiveness and His willingness to cleanse His people of their transgressions.

Perhaps the most profound example of forgiveness in the Old Testament is God's unwavering commitment to forgiving His people, Israel, despite their repeated failures and disobedience. Time and again, the Israelites turned away from God, worshiping idols and breaking the covenant. Yet, God remained faithful, calling them back to repentance and offering forgiveness to those who returned to Him (**Nehemiah 9:16-17**).

The theme of forgiveness in the Old Testament not only reveals the heart of God but also serves as a precursor to the ultimate expression of forgiveness that would be manifested in the coming of Christ. Through these stories and teachings, we see a foreshadowing of the sacrifice that would be made to secure forgiveness for all humanity and the call to extend that same forgiveness to one another.

Chapter 2: New Testament Teachings on Forgiveness

The New Testament builds upon the foundation of forgiveness established in the Old Testament, culminating in the life, teachings, and ultimate sacrifice of Jesus Christ. Throughout the Gospels, forgiveness is a central theme, woven into Christ's words and actions, revealing the depth of God's love and mercy for humanity.

One of the most profound teachings on forgiveness is found in the Lord's Prayer, where Jesus instructs his disciples to pray, "And forgive us our debts, as we also have forgiven our debtors" (**Matthew 6:12**). This simple yet powerful statement establishes a direct link between our ability to receive forgiveness from God and our willingness to extend forgiveness to others. It underscores the reciprocal nature of forgiveness and sets the expectation that those who have been forgiven must, in turn, forgive others.

Jesus reinforced this teaching through powerful parables that illuminated the importance of forgiveness. In the Parable of the Unforgiving Servant (**Matthew 18:21-35**), a servant who had been forgiven an immense debt by his master refused to extend that same forgiveness to a fellow servant who owed him a much smaller amount. This parable serves as a stark warning against the dangers of unforgiveness and the hypocrisy of expecting forgiveness while withholding it from others.

Another powerful illustration of forgiveness is found in the Parable of the Prodigal Son (**Luke 15:11-32**). In this story, a wayward son squanders his inheritance and finds himself destitute and broken. However, when he returns home, his father welcomes him with open arms, celebrating his return and extending unconditional forgiveness. This parable beautifully depicts the depth of God's love and His readiness to forgive those who come to Him in repentance.

Beyond his teachings, Jesus exemplified forgiveness in the most profound way through his sacrifice on the cross. As he was being crucified, he uttered the words, "Father, forgive them, for they do not know what they are doing" (**Luke 23:34**). This act of forgiveness, extended even to those who were responsible for his suffering and death, is a powerful demonstration of the limitless nature of God's mercy and grace.

The apostles, inspired by the teachings and example of Christ, carried the message of forgiveness forward in their writings and ministries. The Apostle Paul, himself a recipient of God's forgiveness, emphasized the importance of extending that same forgiveness to others. In his letter to the Ephesians, he exhorted believers to "be kind to one another, tenderhearted, forgiving one another, as God in Christ forgave you" (**Ephesians 4:32**).

The apostles also recognized forgiveness as a fundamental Christian virtue, essential to the life of a follower of Christ. The Apostle Peter instructed believers to "love one another earnestly from a pure heart" (**1 Peter 1:22**), recognizing that love and forgiveness are inextricably linked. The Apostle John echoed this sentiment, proclaiming, "Beloved, let us love one another, for love is from God, and whoever loves has been born of God and knows God" (**1 John 4:7**).

Through the teachings and example of Jesus Christ and the apostles, the New Testament establishes forgiveness as a cornerstone of the Christian faith. It is not merely a virtuous act but a reflection of the very character of God and a fundamental requirement for those who profess to follow Christ. As we embrace the message of forgiveness, we align ourselves with the heart of God and experience the transformative power of His love and mercy in our own lives and relationships.

Chapter 3: Forgiveness as a Christian Virtue

Throughout the Bible, forgiveness is not only a recurring theme but also a fundamental virtue that is woven into the fabric of the Christian faith. It is a quality that reflects the very character of God and an essential component of living a life that is pleasing to Him.

In the Old Testament, the prophet Micah encapsulated the essence of what it means to live a life that honors God, declaring, "He has told you, O man, what is good; and what does the Lord require of you but to do justice, and to love kindness, and to walk humbly with your God?" **(Micah 6:8)**. Embedded within this exhortation is the call to extend kindness and mercy to others, which is intrinsically tied to the practice of forgiveness.

As we move into the New Testament, forgiveness is elevated to a central tenet of the Christian faith. Jesus himself embodied forgiveness in the most profound way, not only through his teachings but also through his ultimate sacrifice on the cross. By offering himself as the atoning sacrifice for the sins of humanity, Jesus demonstrated the depth of God's forgiveness and set the standard for his followers to emulate.

The Apostle Paul reinforced the importance of forgiveness as a Christian virtue in his letters to the early church. In his epistle to the Colossians, he urged believers to "put on then, as God's chosen ones, holy and beloved, compassionate hearts, kindness, humility, meekness, and patience, bearing with one another and, if one has a complaint against another, forgiving each other; as the Lord has forgiven you, so you also must forgive" **(Colossians 3:12-13)**. Paul recognized that forgiveness is not merely an act but a way of being, a posture of the heart that reflects the character of Christ.

Similarly, the Apostle Peter emphasized the centrality of forgiveness in the life of a believer, exhorting Christians to "have unity of mind, sympathy, brotherly love, a tender heart, and a humble mind" (**1 Peter 3:8**). This call to humility and compassion is directly linked to the practice of forgiveness, as it requires us to let go of pride, bitterness, and the desire for retaliation, and instead extend grace and mercy to those who have wronged us.

Throughout the New Testament, forgiveness is consistently portrayed as a distinguishing mark of a true follower of Christ. Jesus himself declared, "By this all people will know that you are my disciples, if you have love for one another." (**John 13:35**)

Part 3: The Process of Forgiveness
Chapter 1: Letting Go of Anger and Bitterness

The journey towards forgiveness often begins with the acknowledgment and confrontation of the anger and bitterness that reside within our hearts. When we have been wronged or betrayed, it is natural to experience a range of emotions, including hurt, disappointment, and even rage. However, if left unchecked, these powerful emotions can take root and breed a toxic bitterness that can poison our lives and relationships.

The Bible offers wisdom and guidance on the dangers of harboring anger and bitterness. In the book of Ephesians, the Apostle Paul warns believers, "Let all bitterness and wrath and anger and clamor and slander be put away from you, along with all malice" (**Ephesians 4:31**). Paul recognized that bitterness and anger are corrosive forces that can corrupt our hearts and hinder our ability to live in the freedom and joy that Christ intended for us.

Letting go of anger and bitterness is often easier said than done, as these emotions can become deeply entrenched within our psyche. However, it is a crucial step in the process of forgiveness, as holding onto these negative emotions only serves to keep us bound to the offenses of the past and prevents us from moving forward in healing and restoration.

One of the key strategies for letting go of anger and bitterness is to intentionally shift our perspective. Instead of fixating on the hurt and injustice we have experienced, we must strive to view the situation through the lens of compassion and understanding. This does not mean excusing or minimizing the offense, but rather recognizing that all human beings are flawed and capable of making mistakes or causing harm, even unintentionally.

The practice of prayer and meditation can also be powerful tools in the process of letting go. By bringing our hurts and grievances before God, we can find solace and strength to release the burden of anger and bitterness. The Psalms offer a poignant example of this, with the psalmists pouring out their anguish and frustrations to God, ultimately finding peace and resolution through their trust in His love and justice.

Additionally, it is important to recognize that letting go of anger and bitterness is not a one-time event but rather a continuous journey. There may be moments when the feelings of hurt and resentment resurface, and it is in these moments that we must consciously choose to release them once again, trusting in God's grace and the healing power of forgiveness.

Ultimately, letting go of anger and bitterness is a liberating act that frees us from the chains of the past and opens our hearts to the transformative power of forgiveness. As we release these toxic emotions, we create space for healing, restoration, and the cultivation of a spirit of grace and mercy towards those who have wronged us.

Chapter 2: Developing Empathy and Compassion

In the pursuit of forgiveness, the cultivation of empathy and compassion towards the offender is a crucial step. Empathy allows us to step outside of our own perspectives and experiences and attempt to understand the motivations, circumstances, and emotions that may have contributed to the harmful actions of another person.

The Bible offers numerous examples of individuals who demonstrated empathy and compassion, even in the face of great adversity or injustice. One of the most poignant illustrations is found in the life of Joseph, who, despite being betrayed and sold into slavery by his brothers, was able to extend empathy and forgiveness towards them. In **Genesis 45:5**, Joseph declares, "And now do not be distressed or angry with yourselves because you sold me here, for God sent me before you to preserve life." Joseph recognized that his brothers' actions, though wrongful, were ultimately part of a greater plan orchestrated by God.

Another powerful example of empathy and compassion is found in the actions of Jesus Christ. Throughout the Gospels, we witness Jesus extending love, understanding, and forgiveness to those who society had cast aside or condemned. He reached out to tax collectors, sinners, and even those who persecuted and mocked him, demonstrating a depth of empathy and compassion that was truly remarkable.

Developing empathy and compassion requires a conscious effort to see beyond the surface of a person's actions and to consider the various factors that may have contributed to their behavior. It involves acknowledging that all human beings are complex, multifaceted individuals with their own struggles, fears, and vulnerabilities.

One practical way to cultivate empathy and compassion is through active listening and seeking to understand the perspectives and experiences of others. By engaging in open and honest dialogue, we can gain valuable insights into the motivations and circumstances that may have led to the offense or hurt we have experienced.

Additionally, it is important to recognize that empathy and compassion are not contingent upon the offender's remorse or repentance. While repentance can certainly facilitate the forgiveness process, the decision to extend empathy and compassion is one that we make for ourselves, regardless of the actions or responses of the other person.

As we develop empathy and compassion, we begin to see the humanity in those who have wronged us, recognizing that they too are flawed and imperfect beings in need of grace and understanding. This perspective can soften our hearts and create space for forgiveness to take root, allowing us to move forward in the journey of healing and restoration.

Chapter 3: The Role of Repentance

In the journey towards forgiveness, the concept of repentance plays a significant role. Repentance is the acknowledgment and sincere regret for one's wrongdoing, coupled with a genuine desire to change and make amends. While forgiveness can be extended regardless of the offender's repentance, the process of reconciliation and restoration is often facilitated when repentance is present.

The Bible places great emphasis on the importance of repentance, not only in our relationship with God but also in our interactions with others. In the book of Acts, the Apostle Peter exhorts believers to "repent, then, and turn to God, so that your sins may be wiped out" (**Acts 3:19**). This call to repentance is echoed throughout the New Testament, underscoring its crucial role in the forgiveness and restoration process.

Repentance is not merely a verbal acknowledgment of wrongdoing but a heart-felt conviction that leads to a change in behavior and a commitment to making amends where possible. In the context of interpersonal relationships, repentance involves taking responsibility for one's actions, expressing genuine remorse, and actively seeking to repair the damage caused by the offense.

When repentance is present, it can serve as a catalyst for forgiveness, as it demonstrates a willingness to acknowledge the hurt inflicted and a sincere desire to restore the broken relationship. This can help to foster trust and create an environment conducive to the healing process.

However, it is important to note that forgiveness is not contingent upon the offender's repentance. While repentance can facilitate reconciliation, the decision to forgive ultimately rests with the one who has been wronged. The Bible provides examples of individuals who extended forgiveness even in the absence of repentance, such as Jesus forgiving those who crucified him (**Luke 23:34**).

In cases where repentance is not forthcoming, the act of forgiveness becomes an even more powerful expression of grace and mercy. By choosing to forgive regardless of the offender's response, we emulate the unconditional love and forgiveness that God has extended to us through Christ's sacrifice on the cross.

Ultimately, repentance plays a crucial role in the healing and restoration process, but it is not a prerequisite for forgiveness. As followers of Christ, we are called to extend forgiveness freely, recognizing that true repentance is a work of the Holy Spirit in the heart of the offender. By embracing forgiveness, we open the door for reconciliation and create an environment where repentance can take root and flourish.

Chapter 4: Forgiveness as a Decision and Journey

Forgiveness is often portrayed as a single, definitive act – a moment in time when we consciously choose to release the offender from the debt they owe us and let go of the hurt and resentment we have been carrying. While this decision is indeed a crucial step, forgiveness is more accurately understood as a journey, a process that requires ongoing commitment and intentionality.

The Bible offers numerous examples of forgiveness being portrayed as both a decision and a journey. In the Parable of the Prodigal Son (**Luke 15:11-32**), the father's decision to forgive his wayward son is depicted as a single, decisive act of grace and mercy. However, the journey of restoration and reconciliation that followed likely involved ongoing conversations, healing, and the rebuilding of trust over time.

Similarly, in the story of Joseph and his brothers (**Genesis 45:1-15**), Joseph's decision to forgive his brothers for their betrayal is a pivotal moment. However, the true depth and significance of his forgiveness are revealed in the years that followed, as he provided for his family and welcomed them into his life, demonstrating the ongoing nature of forgiveness in action

Part 4: Forgiveness in Relationships
Chapter 1: Forgiveness in Marriage

Marriage is a sacred covenant, a union that binds two individuals together in an intimate partnership of love, trust, and commitment. However, even in the most loving and devoted marriages, offenses and hurts can occur, testing the strength and resilience of the relationship. It is in these moments that the practice of forgiveness becomes paramount, serving as a powerful force for healing, restoration, and growth.

In the Bible, we find numerous examples and teachings that underscore the importance of forgiveness in marriage. The Apostle Paul instructs husbands to "love your wives, just as Christ loved the church and gave himself up for her" (**Ephesians 5:25**). This selfless, sacrificial love is rooted in forgiveness, just as Christ forgave and embraced humanity despite our brokenness and sin.

Forgiveness in marriage requires a willingness to let go of offenses, both big and small. It involves a conscious decision to extend grace and compassion to our spouse, even when they have hurt or disappointed us. This does not mean excusing or minimizing the offense, but rather choosing to release our partner from the debt they owe us and allowing the healing process to begin.

One of the greatest challenges in forgiving our spouse can be the depth of intimacy and vulnerability shared within the marriage relationship. When the person closest to us, the one we have entrusted with our heart and our life, betrays that trust, the pain can be particularly acute. However, it is in these moments that forgiveness becomes even more crucial, as it allows the relationship to move forward and rebuild on a foundation of restored trust and renewed commitment.

Forgiveness in marriage also requires humility and a recognition of our own imperfections. Just as we seek forgiveness from our spouse, we must be willing to extend that same forgiveness when we are the ones who have caused hurt or offense. This mutual practice of forgiveness creates a cycle of grace and understanding that strengthens the marriage bond.

Beyond the interpersonal dynamics, forgiveness in marriage also has a spiritual dimension. When we choose to forgive our spouse, we align our hearts with the heart of God, who has forgiven us through the sacrifice of His Son, Jesus Christ. This act of obedience and submission to God's will can deepen our spiritual intimacy and draw us closer to our Heavenly Father.

Ultimately, forgiveness in marriage is not a one-time event but rather a lifelong journey. As we navigate the challenges and conflicts that inevitably arise in any relationship, the practice of forgiveness becomes a powerful tool for healing, restoring trust, and strengthening the unbreakable bond of matrimony.

Chapter 2: Forgiveness between Parents and Children

The relationship between parents and children is one of the most profound and complex bonds we experience in life. It is a dynamic that is deeply rooted in love, sacrifice, and a desire to nurture and guide the next generation. However, even within this sacred bond, offenses and hurts can occur, testing the resilience and strength of the familial ties.

Forgiveness between parents and children is a two-way street, requiring both parties to extend grace and compassion towards one another. For children, the process of forgiving their parents can be particularly challenging, as the authority and influence that parents hold can make it difficult to let go of perceived wrongs or shortcomings.

In the Bible, we find guidance on the importance of forgiveness within the parent-child relationship. The book of Ephesians instructs children to "honor your father and mother" (**Ephesians 6:2-3**), while also exhorting parents not to "provoke your children to anger, but bring them up in the discipline and instruction of the Lord" (**Ephesians 6:4**). This mutual respect and nurturing love create an environment conducive to forgiveness and reconciliation.

For children, forgiving their parents may involve letting go of resentments or grievances related to perceived failures, emotional wounds, or even abuse or neglect. It is a process that requires vulnerability, courage, and a willingness to extend grace, even when it may seem undeserved. However, by choosing forgiveness, children can find freedom from the burden of bitterness and resentment, allowing them to move forward in their own lives and relationships.

For parents, the practice of forgiveness towards their children is equally important. As the authority figures and guides in their children's lives, parents must model the principles of forgiveness, humility, and grace. This may involve acknowledging their own shortcomings, seeking forgiveness from their children, and creating an environment of open communication and understanding.

Forgiveness between parents and children can also have a profound impact on future generations. When forgiveness is modeled and embraced within the family unit, it creates a legacy of grace and healing that can be passed down to grandchildren and future generations. This generational impact has the power to break cycles of hurt, bitterness, and dysfunction, paving the way for stronger, more resilient family bonds.

Ultimately, forgiveness between parents and children is a journey that requires patience, perseverance, and a willingness to let go of past hurts and grievances. It is a path that leads to deeper understanding, stronger connections, and the opportunity to experience the transformative power of God's love and mercy within the sacred bonds of family.

Chapter 3: Forgiveness in the Church Community

The church is a community of believers, a spiritual family united by their faith in Christ and their commitment to following His teachings. However, even within this sacred fellowship, conflicts, offenses, and hurts can arise, testing the strength and authenticity of the church's commitment to forgiveness and reconciliation.

The Bible is replete with instructions and examples that emphasize the importance of forgiveness within the church community. In **Matthew 18:21-22**, when Peter asks how many times he should forgive his brother, Jesus responds, "I do not say to you seven times, but seventy-seven times." This emphatic statement underscores the limitless nature of forgiveness that should characterize the body of Christ.

The Apostle Paul echoes this sentiment in his letter to the Ephesians, exhorting believers to "be kind to one another, tenderhearted, forgiving one another, as God in Christ forgave you" (**Ephesians 4:32**). This verse highlights the interconnected nature of forgiveness and our relationship with God, reminding us that as we have been forgiven, so too must we extend that same forgiveness to others.

Forgiveness within the church community is not merely a personal matter but a collective responsibility. When offenses or conflicts arise between members, the entire body is affected, and the unity and witness of the church are compromised. It is in these moments that the practice of forgiveness becomes a powerful testimony to the transformative power of the Gospel.

One of the greatest challenges in fostering forgiveness within the church can be the diversity of backgrounds, experiences, and perspectives represented within the congregation. Differences in culture, upbringing, and personal histories can create misunderstandings and miscommunications that can lead to hurt and offense. However, it is through the practice of forgiveness that these differences can be bridged and a true sense of unity and belonging can be cultivated.

Forgiveness within the church community also requires humility and a willingness to acknowledge one's own imperfections and shortcomings. As members of the body of Christ, we are all called to walk in humility, recognizing that we are all in need of God's grace and forgiveness. This mindset creates an environment where forgiveness can flourish, as we extend the same mercy and understanding to others that we ourselves have received from God.

Ultimately, forgiveness within the church community is not just a matter of maintaining harmony and avoiding conflict; it is a reflection of the very heart of the Gospel message. When we forgive one another, we bear witness to the transformative power of Christ's love and sacrifice, embodying the principles of grace, mercy, and reconciliation that lie at the core of our faith.

Chapter 4: Forgiveness in the Workplace

The workplace is often a microcosm of the broader society, bringing together individuals from diverse backgrounds, cultures, and belief systems. Within this dynamic environment, conflicts, misunderstandings, and offenses are virtually inevitable, making the practice of forgiveness a crucial component of a healthy and productive work culture.

In the Bible, we find numerous examples and teachings that underscore the importance of forgiveness in our professional and work-related relationships. The book of Proverbs instructs, "A gentle answer turns away wrath, but a harsh word stirs up anger" (**Proverbs 15:1**). This wisdom highlights the power of a forgiving and measured response in diffusing conflict and promoting understanding in the workplace.

The Apostle Paul's teachings also provide guidance on the importance of forgiveness in our interactions with others, including those we may work alongside. In his letter to the Colossians, he exhorts believers to "put on then, as God's chosen ones, holy and beloved, compassionate hearts, kindness, humility, meekness, and patience, bearing with one another and, if one has a complaint against another, forgiving each other; as the Lord has forgiven you, so you also must forgive.

Part 5: Cultivating a Forgiving Heart
Chapter 1: Imitating God's Forgiveness

At the heart of the Christian faith lies the profound truth that God is a God of forgiveness. From the very beginning, when sin first entered the world through the disobedience of Adam and Eve, God extended the promise of redemption and forgiveness (**Genesis 3:15**). Throughout the narrative of Scripture, we see God's steadfast love and mercy toward His people, even in the face of their repeated rebellion and unfaithfulness.

In the Old Testament, we witness God's forgiveness extended to the nation of Israel time and again. After their deliverance from Egyptian bondage, the Israelites repeatedly turned away from God, worshiping idols and breaking the covenant. Yet, God remained faithful, calling them back to repentance and offering forgiveness to those who returned to Him (**Nehemiah 9:16-17**).

The ultimate expression of God's forgiveness is found in the person of Jesus Christ. In one of the most powerful verses in Scripture, the Apostle Paul declares, "But God demonstrates His own love toward us, in that while we were yet sinners, Christ died for us" (**Romans 5:8**). Through the sacrifice of His Son, God extended forgiveness to all humanity, offering the gift of salvation and eternal life to those who place their faith in Christ.

Jesus not only exemplified forgiveness through his death on the cross but also through his teachings and interactions with others. In the parable of the Prodigal Son (**Luke 15:11-32**), Jesus illustrates the depth of God's forgiveness, depicting the father's joyful acceptance of his wayward son upon his return. Jesus himself modeled forgiveness in the most profound way when, as he was being crucified, he uttered the words, "Father, forgive them, for they do not know what they are doing" (**Luke 23:34**).

As followers of Christ, we are called to imitate God's forgiveness in our own lives. Just as God has forgiven us, we are to extend that same forgiveness to others (**Ephesians 4:32**). This is not an easy task, as forgiveness often goes against our natural inclinations for justice and retribution. However, when we forgive others, we align our hearts with the heart of God, reflecting His character and demonstrating the transformative power of His love.

Imitating God's forgiveness requires a conscious decision to let go of bitterness, resentment, and the desire for vengeance. It involves a willingness to see others through the lens of compassion and grace, recognizing our own need for forgiveness. As we extend forgiveness to those who have wronged us, we not only free them from the debt they owe us but also liberate ourselves from the burden of unforgiveness.

Chapter 2: The Healing Power of Forgiveness

Forgiveness is not merely a spiritual concept or a moral obligation; it is also a powerful force for healing and restoration. When we choose to forgive, we open the door to a journey of personal growth, emotional freedom, and spiritual renewal.

On a personal level, forgiveness has the power to heal deep emotional wounds and lift the heavy burden of bitterness and resentment. By letting go of the anger and hurt that accompanies unforgiveness, we create space for peace, joy, and emotional well-being to flourish within our hearts and minds.

Numerous studies have shown the positive impact of forgiveness on mental and physical health. Individuals who practice forgiveness tend to experience lower levels of anxiety, depression, and stress, as well as improved sleep patterns and overall well-being. Conversely, harboring unforgiveness and bitterness has been linked to a host of negative health consequences, including increased risk of heart disease, high blood pressure, and compromised immune function.

Forgiveness also has the power to heal relationships that have been fractured by wrongdoing or betrayal. When we extend forgiveness to those who have hurt us, we create an opportunity for reconciliation and restoration. While forgiveness does not automatically repair the relationship or erase the consequences of the offense, it lays the foundation for healing and the potential for a renewed, healthier dynamic.

In families and communities, forgiveness can break cycles of hurt, resentment, and division that can span generations. By choosing to forgive, we disrupt the destructive patterns of retaliation and bitterness, paving the way for understanding, empathy, and unity.

Ultimately, forgiveness has the power to heal our relationship with God. When we harbor unforgiveness towards others, it hinders our ability to fully embrace and experience the forgiveness that God has extended to us through Christ. By letting go of our grievances and aligning our hearts with God's heart of forgiveness, we open ourselves to the healing and restoration that can only come through a deep, intimate connection with our Heavenly Father.

The Bible is replete with examples of the healing power of forgiveness. In the book of Genesis, we witness the profound reconciliation between Joseph and his brothers, a story that illustrates the transformative impact of forgiveness on relationships and families (**Genesis 45:1-15**). The Apostle Paul's own life is a testament to the healing power of forgiveness, as he went from being a persecutor of the early Church to becoming one of its most influential leaders and missionaries (**Acts 9:1-22**).

Chapter 3: Forgiveness as a Lifestyle

Forgiveness is not a one-time event or a single decision; it is a lifestyle, a way of being that permeates every aspect of our existence. To truly embrace forgiveness is to adopt a posture of humility, grace, and compassion towards others, recognizing our own need for forgiveness and extending that same mercy to those around us.

Living a lifestyle of forgiveness requires a continual commitment to letting go of offenses, both big and small. It means actively choosing not to hold onto grudges or harbor resentment, even when the temptation to do so is strong. This is not an easy task, as the human heart naturally gravitates towards self-preservation and the desire for retribution.

The Apostle Paul encourages believers to "put on then, as God's chosen ones, holy and beloved, compassionate hearts, kindness, humility, meekness, and patience, bearing with one another and, if one has a complaint against another, forgiving each other; as the Lord has forgiven you, so you also must forgive" (**Colossians 3:12-13**). This exhortation highlights the interconnected nature of forgiveness and other virtues such as compassion, kindness, and humility, underscoring the reality that forgiveness is not merely an isolated act but a way of life.

Adopting a lifestyle of forgiveness requires a mindset shift, a conscious decision to view others through the lens of grace and mercy, just as God has extended grace and mercy to us. It means being quick to forgive and slow to take offense, recognizing that we all fall short and are in need of forgiveness ourselves.

Living a forgiving life also involves cultivating a spirit of humility and self-awareness. When we recognize our own imperfections and shortcomings, it becomes easier to extend grace and understanding to others who stumble or fall short. The acknowledgment of our own need for forgiveness serves as a powerful catalyst for extending that same forgiveness to those around us.

Ultimately, embracing forgiveness as a lifestyle is a reflection of our relationship with Christ and our desire to emulate His character. Jesus embodied a life of forgiveness, consistently extending grace and mercy to those around Him, even in the face of betrayal and rejection. As His followers, we are called to walk in His footsteps, allowing the transformative power of forgiveness to permeate every aspect of our lives.

Chapter 4: Overcoming Obstacles to Forgiveness

While the call to forgiveness is clear, the journey towards embracing it is often fraught with obstacles and challenges. These hurdles can stem from our own internal struggles, the nature of the offense committed against us, or the response (**or lack thereof**) from the offender. However, by acknowledging and addressing these obstacles, we can find the strength and courage to press forward in the pursuit of forgiveness.

One of the most significant obstacles to forgiveness is the depth of the hurt or betrayal we have experienced. When the wound is profound, it can be incredibly difficult to let go of the anger, bitterness, and desire for retribution that accompany it. In such cases, it is crucial to acknowledge the validity of our pain and allow ourselves to grieve the loss or damage inflicted upon us.

Another obstacle can be the lack of repentance or remorse from the offender. When someone has wronged us and shows no genuine contrition or acknowledgment of their actions, it can feel like an act of futility to extend forgiveness. However, it is important to remember that forgiveness is ultimately a choice we make for ourselves, not contingent upon the response or actions of the offender.

Pride and a stubborn refusal to let go of our grievances can also hinder our ability to forgive. We may cling to the belief that we are justified in our anger or that forgiveness is a sign of weakness.

Chapter 1: Forgiveness as the Way of Christ

Throughout this journey of exploration, one resounding truth has become abundantly clear: forgiveness is not merely a virtuous act or a noble ideal; it is the very heart and essence of the Christian faith. It is the way of Christ, the path that He walked and the example He set for all who would follow in His footsteps.

From the moment sin entered the world, God's plan for redemption and forgiveness was set in motion. Through the narratives of the Old Testament, we witness glimpses of this divine plan, as God extended mercy and forgiveness to His people time and again, even in the face of their repeated disobedience and rebellion.

However, it was in the life, teachings, and ultimate sacrifice of Jesus Christ that the fullness of God's forgiveness was revealed. In His interactions with sinners, tax collectors, and those cast aside by society, Jesus modeled a radical posture of compassion, grace, and forgiveness. He challenged the religious establishment of His day, extending love and acceptance to those they had condemned and rejected.

In the Parable of the Prodigal Son, Jesus painted a vivid picture of the depth of God's forgiveness, depicting a father who joyfully welcomes back his wayward son, celebrating his return and restoring him to his rightful place in the family. This parable serves as a powerful illustration of the unconditional love and forgiveness that God extends to all who come to Him in repentance and humility.

Yet, it was on the cross that Jesus' forgiveness reached its ultimate expression. As He endured the agony and humiliation of crucifixion, He uttered the words, "Father, forgive them, for they do not know what they are doing" (Luke 23:34). In that moment, Jesus exemplified the boundless nature of God's mercy, extending forgiveness even to those who were responsible for His suffering and death.

The apostles, inspired by the teachings and example of Christ, carried this message of forgiveness forward, urging believers to "be kind to one another, tenderhearted, forgiving one another, as God in Christ forgave you" (Ephesians 4:32). They recognized forgiveness not merely as a virtuous act but as a fundamental requirement for those who call themselves followers of Christ.

As we reflect on the life and ministry of Jesus, it becomes evident that forgiveness was not simply a peripheral teaching or an optional practice; it was the very essence of His mission, the heart of the Gospel message. To follow in His footsteps is to embrace forgiveness as a way of life, a posture of the heart that reflects the character and love of our Heavenly Father.

Chapter 2: The Transformative Impact of Forgiveness

Forgiveness is not merely a spiritual concept or a moral imperative; it is a powerful force capable of transforming lives, relationships, and entire communities. Throughout this book, we have explored the profound impact that forgiveness can have on both a personal and societal level, revealing its ability to heal wounds, restore broken bonds, and break cycles of hurt and retaliation.

On a personal level, forgiveness offers the promise of emotional freedom and healing. When we choose to let go of anger, bitterness, and resentment, we liberate ourselves from the burden of carrying those toxic emotions. Forgiveness creates space for peace, joy, and emotional well-being to flourish within our hearts and minds, allowing us to experience the fullness of life that Christ intended for us.

Numerous studies have also shown the positive impact of forgiveness on mental and physical health. Individuals who practice forgiveness tend to experience lower levels of anxiety, depression, and stress, as well as improved sleep patterns and overall well-being. Conversely, harboring unforgiveness and bitterness has been linked to a host of negative health consequences, including increased risk of heart disease, high blood pressure, and compromised immune function.

In relationships, forgiveness serves as a powerful force for restoration and reconciliation. When we extend forgiveness to those who have hurt or betrayed us, we create an opportunity for broken bonds to be mended and trust to be rebuilt. Forgiveness paves the way for understanding, empathy, and the potential for deeper, more authentic connections.

Within families and communities, forgiveness has the capacity to break cycles of hurt, resentment, and division that can span generations. By choosing to forgive, we disrupt the destructive patterns of retaliation and bitterness, paving the way for unity, healing, and a renewed sense of belonging.

Ultimately, forgiveness has the power to transform not only individuals but entire societies. Throughout history, we have witnessed the transformative impact of forgiveness on a larger scale, as individuals and movements have embraced the principles of non-violence, reconciliation, and restorative justice. From the civil rights movement led by Dr. Martin Luther King Jr. to the truth and reconciliation processes in post-apartheid South Africa, forgiveness has proven to be a powerful catalyst for societal change and healing.

As we reflect on the transformative impact of forgiveness, we are reminded of the profound words of Nelson Mandela, who said, "Forgiveness liberates the soul. It removes fear. That is why it is such a powerful weapon." Forgiveness is not merely a noble ideal or a virtuous act; it is a force that has the power to change lives, mend relationships, and shape the course of history itself.

Chapter 3: Call to a Life of Forgiveness

As we conclude this journey through the steadfast perspective of the human heart on forgiveness, we are confronted with a profound call – a call to embrace forgiveness as a way of life, a posture of the heart that permeates every aspect of our existence.

This call is not merely a suggestion or a piece of well-intentioned advice; it is a mandate rooted in the very teachings and example of Jesus Christ. Throughout the Gospels, we witness Christ embodying forgiveness in the most radical and transformative way, extending grace, mercy, and love to those who had wronged Him and defying the societal norms of His day.

In the Sermon on the Mount, Jesus declared, "Blessed are the merciful, for they shall receive mercy" (Matthew 5:7). These words serve as a powerful reminder that forgiveness is not only a virtue to be admired but a fundamental requirement for those who seek to follow in the footsteps of Christ.

The apostles echoed this call, urging believers to "put on then, as God's chosen ones, holy and beloved, compassionate hearts, kindness, humility, meekness, and patience, bearing with one another and, if one has a complaint against another, forgiving each other; as the Lord has forgiven you, so you also must forgive" **(Colossians 3:12-13)**. This exhortation reminds us that forgiveness is not an optional practice but an essential component of the Christian life.

Embracing a life of forgiveness requires a fundamental shift in our perspective and a willingness to let go of the natural human inclinations towards bitterness, resentment, and the desire for retaliation. It involves cultivating a posture of humility, recognizing our own need for forgiveness and extending that same grace and mercy to those who have wronged us.

Living a life of forgiveness is not without its challenges. It requires a conscious effort to overcome the obstacles that stand in our way, whether they be the depth of the hurt we have experienced, the lack of repentance from the offender, or our own stubborn pride. However, as we have explored throughout this book, the rewards of forgiveness far outweigh the difficulties of the journey.

Ultimately, the call to a life of forgiveness is a call to align our hearts with the very heart of God, who has extended boundless forgiveness to us through the sacrifice of His Son, Jesus Christ. It is a call to reflect the character of Christ in our interactions with others, to be agents of healing, restoration, and reconciliation in a world that desperately needs the transformative power of forgiveness.

As we step forward into this new chapter, may we embrace the words of the Apostle Paul, who declared, "Therefore, if anyone is in Christ, he is a new creation. The old has passed away; behold, the new has come" (2 Corinthians 5:17). May we be new creations, defined not by the hurts and offenses of the past, but by the grace and mercy that flow from a life surrendered to the way of forgiveness – the way of Christ.

Chapter 4: The Blessing of a Forgiving Spirit

As we conclude this comprehensive exploration of forgiveness from a biblical perspective, we are confronted with a profound truth: cultivating a forgiving spirit is not merely a virtuous act or a noble aspiration; it is a profound blessing that has the power to transform our lives and relationships in ways that transcend our limited human understanding.

Throughout the pages of this book, we have witnessed the transformative impact of forgiveness in action. We have seen how it has the power to heal deep emotional wounds, restore broken relationships, and break cycles of hurt and bitterness that have spanned generations. We have explored the biblical foundations of forgiveness, tracing its roots through the narratives of the Old and New Testaments, and witnessing its ultimate embodiment in the life, teachings, and sacrifice of Jesus Christ.

Yet, beyond the practical and spiritual benefits of forgiveness, there is a deeper blessing that awaits those who embrace a forgiving spirit – a blessing that touches the very essence of our being and our connection to the heart of God.

When we choose to forgive, we align our hearts with the heart of our Heavenly Father, who has extended boundless forgiveness to us through the sacrifice of His Son. We reflect the very character of Christ, who modeled forgiveness in the most radical and transformative way, extending grace and mercy even to those who crucified Him.

In cultivating a forgiving spirit, we experience a profound freedom – a liberation from the chains of bitterness, resentment, and the desire for retaliation that so often weigh heavily upon the human soul. We are freed from the burden of carrying the offenses and hurts of the past, allowing us to embrace the present moment with a lightness of spirit and a renewed sense of purpose.

Moreover, a forgiving spirit opens our hearts to the deeper mysteries of God's love and grace. When we extend forgiveness to those who have wronged us, we catch a glimpse of the unfathomable mercy that God has shown us, despite our own failings and transgressions. We are humbled by the realization that we, too, are recipients of a forgiveness that we could never fully earn or deserve, and this humility draws us closer to the heart of our Heavenly Father.

In this posture of forgiveness, we experience a profound sense of peace – a peace that surpasses human understanding and transcends the circumstances of our lives. It is a peace that flows from the knowledge that we are loved, accepted, and forgiven by a God who is infinitely merciful and compassionate.

Additionally, a forgiving spirit cultivates a spirit of gratitude within us. As we reflect on the depths of God's forgiveness towards us, we are filled with a profound sense of thankfulness for the grace that has been extended to us, despite our unworthiness. This gratitude becomes a wellspring of joy, sustaining us through the trials and challenges of life and shaping our perspective on even the most difficult of circumstances.

Ultimately, the blessing of a forgiving spirit is the blessing of drawing closer to the heart of God Himself. It is a journey that leads us to a deeper understanding of His character, a more intimate relationship with Him, and a greater appreciation for the sacrificial love that was displayed on the cross of Calvary.

As we embrace this forgiving spirit, we become vessels of God's grace and mercy in a world that desperately needs to experience the transformative power of forgiveness. We become agents of healing, reconciliation, and restoration, reflecting the light of Christ in the darkest corners of our broken world.

So, let us step forward into this new chapter with hearts open to the blessing of a forgiving spirit. Let us embrace the words of the Apostle Paul, who declared, "And we know that for those who love God all things work together for good, for those who are called according to his purpose" (**Romans 8:28**) May our forgiving spirits bear witness to the goodness and faithfulness of our God, and may we experience the fullness of His blessings as we walk in the way of forgiveness – the way of Christ.

Chapter 5: Forgiveness as a Pathway to Wholeness

As we have journeyed through the richness of Scripture and explored the profound truths surrounding forgiveness, a clear reality emerges: embracing forgiveness is not merely a virtuous act or a noble aspiration; it is a transformative pathway that leads us toward wholeness – a wholeness of spirit, mind, and relationships.

In the pages of the Bible, we encounter countless stories of individuals who experienced the healing and restorative power of forgiveness. From Joseph, who forgave his brothers for their betrayal, to the thief on the cross, who received forgiveness from Christ in his final moments, these narratives bear witness to the profound impact that forgiveness can have on the human soul.

When we choose to forgive, we open ourselves to the transformative work of God's grace in our lives. We allow the power of the cross to penetrate the deepest recesses of our hearts, where wounds and resentments have taken root, and we invite the healing balm of forgiveness to bring restoration and wholeness.

Forgiveness has the power to mend the brokenness within us, healing the emotional and psychological scars left by the offenses and hurts we have endured. As we release the burden of bitterness and resentment, we create space for peace, joy, and emotional well-being to flourish within our souls. We experience a lightness of spirit and a freedom that transcends the circumstances of our lives.

Moreover, forgiveness paves the way for the restoration of our relationships, both with God and with others. When we extend forgiveness to those who have wronged us, we dismantle the barriers that have erected and allow for the possibility of reconciliation and the rebuilding of trust. Forgiveness creates an environment where healing can take root and where broken bonds can be mended.

In our relationship with God, forgiveness plays a crucial role in our spiritual wholeness. As we accept the forgiveness that God has extended to us through the sacrifice of His Son, Jesus Christ, we experience a profound sense of freedom and a deeper understanding of His love and grace. We are liberated from the weight of guilt and shame, and we are empowered to walk in the fullness of our identity as beloved children of God.

Furthermore, forgiveness has the power to break generational cycles of hurt, bitterness, and dysfunction. When we choose to forgive, we disrupt the destructive patterns that have been passed down through generations, paving the way for a legacy of healing, reconciliation, and wholeness.

As we embrace forgiveness as a pathway to wholeness, we align ourselves with the very heart of God – a heart that is characterized by mercy, compassion, and an unwavering commitment to restoration. We reflect the image of Christ, who embodied forgiveness in the most radical and transformative way, extending grace and mercy even to those who crucified Him.

Ultimately, forgiveness is not merely a noble virtue or a spiritual discipline; it is a journey that leads us toward the fullness of life that Christ promised. It is a pathway that invites us to experience the wholeness of spirit, mind, and relationships that can only be found in the embrace of God's forgiveness and the extension of that same forgiveness to others.

Chapter 6: Forgiveness as a Catalyst for Societal Transformation

While forgiveness is often viewed through the lens of personal healing and restoration, its impact extends far beyond the individual realm. Forgiveness has the power to catalyze societal transformation, breaking down barriers of division, fostering reconciliation, and paving the way for a more just and equitable world.

Throughout history, we have witnessed the transformative power of forgiveness on a societal scale. Movements that have embraced the principles of non-violence, restorative justice, and forgiveness have profoundly impacted the trajectory of nations and communities, offering a path forward in the face of seemingly insurmountable conflicts and injustices.

One of the most powerful examples of forgiveness's societal impact can be found in the life and legacy of Dr. Martin Luther King Jr. and the civil rights movement. In the face of oppression, violence, and systemic racism, Dr. King championed a philosophy of none violent resistance rooted in the principles of love and forgiveness. His unwavering commitment to these ideals inspired a nation and catalyzed a movement that ultimately toppled the unjust system of segregation and discrimination.

Similarly, the truth and reconciliation process in post-apartheid South Africa stands as a testament to the transformative power of forgiveness on a national scale. After decades of oppression, violence, and racial injustice, the nation embarked on a journey of healing and reconciliation, centered on the principles of forgiveness, truth-telling, and restorative justice. This process, while imperfect, laid the foundation for a more unified and equitable society, demonstrating the potential for forgiveness to bridge even the deepest divides.

In the realm of restorative justice, forgiveness has proven to be a powerful force for transforming the way we approach crime, punishment, and rehabilitation. Restorative justice initiatives, which emphasize accountability, victim-offender dialogue, and the restoration of relationships, have yielded promising results in reducing recidivism rates and fostering a greater sense of healing and closure for victims and offenders alike.

At its core, forgiveness has the power to disrupt cycles of violence, retaliation, and perpetual conflict that have plagued societies throughout history. When individuals and communities embrace forgiveness, they create space for dialogue, understanding, and the possibility of reconciliation – elements that are essential for building a more just, equitable, and peaceful world.

Furthermore, forgiveness has the capacity to challenge and transform deeply entrenched systems of oppression, injustice, and marginalization. When those who have been oppressed or victimized choose to extend forgiveness, they reclaim their dignity and humanity, refusing to be defined by the actions of their oppressors. This act of forgiveness strips away the power and legitimacy of unjust systems, creating a pathway for meaningful change and reform.

Ultimately, forgiveness is not merely a personal virtue or a spiritual discipline; it is a powerful force that can shape the trajectory of entire societies. When individuals and communities embrace forgiveness, they unleash a transformative energy that has the potential to break down barriers, heal wounds, and pave the way for a more just, equitable, and peaceful world.

Chapter 7: Forgiveness as a Reflection of Divine Grace

At the heart of forgiveness lies a profound truth – one that reflects the very essence of the Christian faith and the character of God Himself. Forgiveness is not merely a virtuous act or a noble aspiration; it is a reflection of the divine grace that has been extended to us through the sacrifice of Jesus Christ.

From the very beginning, when sin first entered the world, God's plan for redemption and forgiveness was set in motion. Through the narratives of the Old Testament, we witness glimpses of this divine plan, as God extends mercy and forgiveness to His people time and again, even in the face of their repeated disobedience and rebellion.

However, it is in the life, teachings, and ultimate sacrifice of Jesus Christ that the fullness of God's forgiveness is revealed. In His interactions with sinners, tax collectors, and those cast aside by society, Jesus modeled a radical posture of compassion, grace, and forgiveness. He challenged the religious establishment of His day, extending love and acceptance to those they had condemned and rejected.

On the cross, Jesus' forgiveness reached its ultimate expression. As He endured the agony and humiliation of crucifixion, He uttered the words, "Father, forgive them, for they do not know what they are doing" (**Luke 23:34**). In that moment, Jesus exemplified the boundless nature of God's mercy, extending forgiveness even to those who were responsible for His suffering and death.

The apostles, inspired by the teachings and example of Christ, carried this message of forgiveness forward, urging believers to "be kind to one another, tenderhearted, forgiving one another, as God in Christ forgave you" (**Ephesians 4:32**). They recognized forgiveness not merely as a virtuous act but as a fundamental requirement for those who call themselves followers of Christ.

When we choose to forgive, we reflect the very character of God – a character defined by love, mercy, and an unwavering commitment to restoration. We emulate the heart of our Heavenly Father, who has extended boundless forgiveness to us, despite our own failings and transgressions.

Forgiveness is not merely a human endeavor; it is a divine invitation to participate in the redemptive work of God. As we forgive others, we become vessels of God's grace, channels through which His love and mercy flow into a broken and hurting world.

Moreover, forgiveness serves as a powerful testimony to the transformative power of the Gospel. When we extend forgiveness to those who have wronged us, we bear witness to the reality that true transformation is possible – that even the deepest wounds and most seemingly insurmountable barriers can be overcome through the power of God's grace.

Ultimately, forgiveness is a reflection of the divine grace that has been lavished upon us through the sacrifice of Christ.

Chapter 8: Forgiveness as a Source of Strength

As we journey through the complexities of life, with its inevitable challenges, disappointments, and hurts, the practice of forgiveness emerges as a wellspring of strength – a source of resilience that empowers us to rise above the circumstances that threaten to weigh us down.

In a world that often celebrates retaliation, vengeance, and the pursuit of personal vindication, forgiveness stands as a countercultural force, a testament to the power of grace and mercy to overcome even the most profound injustices and betrayals.

The strength found in forgiveness is not born of weakness or capitulation; rather, it stems from a deep inner resolve, a recognition that holding onto bitterness and resentment ultimately serves no purpose other than to corrode the soul and hinder personal growth and healing.

When we choose to forgive, we reclaim our power over the offenses and hurts that have been inflicted upon us. We refuse to allow the actions of others to define us or dictate the trajectory of our lives. Instead, we embrace forgiveness as a courageous act of self-determination, a declaration that we will not be held captive by the weight of past grievances.

In the midst of personal struggles, family conflicts, or societal injustices, forgiveness becomes a source of hope – a beacon that illuminates the path forward, even when the way seems shrouded in darkness. It reminds us that healing and restoration are possible, that broken relationships can be mended, and that even the deepest wounds can be transformed into sources of wisdom and growth.

Moreover, forgiveness is a wellspring of spiritual strength, drawing us closer to the heart of God and aligning our hearts with His character of mercy and grace. As we extend forgiveness to others, we participate in the redemptive work of Christ, reflecting the unconditional love that was displayed on the cross of Calvary.

The strength found in forgiveness is not merely an abstract concept; it is a tangible force that has the power to transform lives, relationships, and entire communities. Throughout history, we have witnessed individuals and movements that have drawn upon the strength of forgiveness to overcome seemingly insurmountable obstacles and catalyze lasting change.

In the face of adversity, forgiveness becomes a source of resilience, enabling us to weather the storms of life with a spirit of grace and compassion. It empowers us to rise above the petty grievances and hurts that so often consume our energy and attention, liberating us to focus on what truly matters – living a life of purpose, love, and service to others.

Ultimately, forgiveness is a source of strength that flows from the very heart of God – a strength that transcends our limited human understanding and enables us to walk in the fullness of the life that Christ promised. As we embrace the practice of forgiveness, we tap into a wellspring of power that has the potential to transform our lives, our relationships, and the world around us.

Chapter 9: Forgiveness as a Legacy for Future Generations

As we navigate the complexities of life and grapple with the hurts and injustices that inevitably come our way, it is imperative that we consider not only the present moment but also the impact our choices will have on future generations. Forgiveness, in this context, emerges as a powerful legacy – a gift that we can bestow upon our children, grandchildren, and the generations yet to come.

Throughout history, we have witnessed the devastating consequences of unforgiveness, bitterness, and generational trauma. Cycles of violence, retaliation, and perpetual conflict have plagued families, communities, and entire nations, perpetuating a legacy of pain and brokenness that spans generations.

However, when we choose to embrace forgiveness, we disrupt these cycles and create a new legacy – one rooted in healing, restoration, and the transformative power of grace and mercy.

By modeling forgiveness in our relationships, we teach our children the invaluable lessons of compassion, empathy, and the ability to let go of grievances. We demonstrate that true strength lies not in holding onto bitterness but in the courage to extend grace and understanding, even in the face of profound hurt or betrayal.

When children witness forgiveness in action, they learn that conflicts and offenses need not define their lives or dictate the trajectory of their relationships. They come to understand that healing and reconciliation are possible, and that the bonds of family and community can be mended, even in the aftermath of deep wounds.

Moreover, forgiveness has the power to liberate future generations from the burden of inherited resentments and grievances. By choosing to break the cycles of unforgiveness, we free our descendants from the weight of carrying forward the hurts and injustices of the past. We create a clean slate, a fresh start, where they can forge their own paths unencumbered by the baggage of generational trauma.

In families and communities where forgiveness is embraced, a culture of grace and understanding takes root – a culture that celebrates the dignity and worth of every individual and fosters an environment of mutual respect and compassion. This legacy has the potential to shape the worldview and values of future generations, equipping them to navigate life's challenges with a spirit of resilience, empathy, and a commitment to building a more just and equitable society.

Furthermore, forgiveness serves as a powerful testimony of faith – a living example of the transformative power of the Gospel and the boundless mercy that God has extended to us through the sacrifice of His Son, Jesus Christ. By embracing forgiveness, we bear witness to the reality that true redemption and restoration are possible, even in the face of the most profound brokenness and pain.

Ultimately, forgiveness is a legacy that transcends the temporal and echoes into eternity. It is a gift that we can bestow upon our children and future generations – a legacy of healing, reconciliation, and the unwavering belief that love and grace have the power to overcome even the darkest of circumstances. As we embrace forgiveness, we sow seeds of hope and transformation that will bear fruit for generations to come.

Chapter 10: Forgiveness as a Catalyst for Personal Renewal

In the journey of life, there are moments when we find ourselves at a crossroads – seasons of transition, growth, and the opportunity for personal renewal. It is in these pivotal moments that the practice of forgiveness emerges as a powerful catalyst, propelling us forward on a path of transformation and spiritual growth.

When we carry the weight of past hurts, grievances, and unresolved conflicts, we inevitably become weighed down by the baggage of unforgiveness. This burden can hinder our ability to fully embrace the present moment and step into the fullness of the life that God has called us to live.

However, when we choose to forgive, we lighten the load and create space for personal renewal and growth. By letting go of the resentments and bitterness that have held us captive, we open ourselves up to the transformative work of the Holy Spirit, allowing God's grace and mercy to penetrate the deepest recesses of our hearts and minds.

Forgiveness has the power to liberate us from the cycles of shame, guilt, and self-condemnation that so often accompany the wounds of the past. As we extend forgiveness to others and receive the forgiveness that God has extended to us, we experience a profound sense of freedom – a freedom that empowers us to shed the limiting beliefs and self-imposed barriers that have hindered our spiritual growth.

In the crucible of forgiveness, we are refined and shaped into vessels of God's love and grace. We emerge with a renewed sense of purpose, a deeper understanding of our identity in Christ, and a heightened awareness of the calling that God has placed upon our lives.

Furthermore, forgiveness serves as a catalyst for personal renewal by fostering a spirit of humility and gratitude within us. As we reflect on the depths of God's forgiveness towards us, we are humbled by the realization that we, too, have been recipients of a mercy and grace that we could never fully earn or deserve. This humility cultivates a heart of thankfulness, which becomes a wellspring of joy and strength, sustaining us through the challenges and transitions that lie ahead.

Ultimately, forgiveness is not merely a virtuous act or a spiritual discipline; it is a transformative force that has the power to reshape our lives and propel us forward on a journey of personal renewal and spiritual growth. As we embrace forgiveness, we align ourselves with the heart of God and participate in the redemptive work of Christ, allowing His love and grace to permeate every aspect of our being.

In the seasons of transition and growth, forgiveness emerges as a catalyst, igniting a flame of transformation within us – a flame that burns away the dross of the past and refines us into vessels fit for the Master's use. As we step into this journey of personal renewal, may we cling to the words of the Apostle Paul, who declared, "Therefore, if anyone is in Christ, he is a new creation. The old has passed away; behold, the new has come" (**2 Corinthians 5:17**). May forgiveness be the catalyst that propels us into the fullness of this new life, empowering us to embrace the calling and purpose that God has ordained for each of us.

As you conclude this journey through the pages of this book, reflecting on the steadfast perspective of the human heart on forgiveness, may you be filled with a renewed sense of hope and determination. The path of forgiveness is not an easy one, but it is a path that leads to freedom, healing, and the transformative power of God's grace.

Remember that forgiveness is not a one-time event but a daily choice, a lifestyle that requires intentionality and perseverance. There will be moments when the sting of pasts hurts resurfaces, tempting you to hold onto bitterness and resentment. In those moments, lean into the

truths you have learned – truths about the boundless mercy of God, the healing power of forgiveness, and the strength that comes from letting go.

Forgiveness is not a sign of weakness; it is a courageous act that requires great inner resolve and a willingness to step out of the comfort zone of anger and retaliation. But as you take those steps, you will discover a freedom and lightness of spirit that transcends your circumstances.

Remember that forgiveness is not contingent upon the response or actions of the offender. It is a choice you make for yourself, a decision to release the burden of unforgiveness and embrace the peace and joy that come from aligning your heart with the heart of God.

As you navigate the complexities of relationships and the inevitable hurts that come with human interactions, let forgiveness be your guide. Forgive quickly and freely, not allowing offenses to take root and breed bitterness. Cultivate a spirit of empathy, compassion, and grace, remembering that you, too, have been the recipient of God's forgiveness through the sacrifice of His Son, Jesus Christ.

And when the journey seems too difficult, when the wounds feel too deep or the offenses too great, turn your gaze to the cross. There, you will find the ultimate example of forgiveness – a love so profound, so boundless, that it extends mercy and grace even to those responsible for the suffering and death of the Savior Himself.

May the words and truths within this book be a constant source of encouragement and strength as you embrace the daily practice of forgiveness. And may the power of God's love and mercy flow through you, transforming your heart, your relationships, and the world around you – one act of forgiveness at a time.

Remember, forgiveness is not just a virtuous act; it is the way of Christ, the path to wholeness, and the key to unlocking the abundant life He promised. So go forth, forgive freely, and bear witness to the transformative power of grace and mercy in a world that desperately needs to experience the healing balm of forgiveness.

Shawn Felton

Did you love *The Unforgiving Heart*? Then you should read *Yahweh & Clyde: Forward Into Salvation*[1] by SHAWN FELTON!

[2]

"Yahweh and Clyde :Forward into Salvation"

In a world where morality is often seen as outdated and restrictive, one man's journey proves that ancient wisdom may be the key to modern redemption.

Clyde is a man at war with himself. He's crumbling within - trapped in a cycle of lies, greed, and deceit. His life is a sham, his career built on lies, and his soul crying out for something more.

When Clyde stumbles upon the Ten Commandments, he dismisses them as old rules with no place in his 21st-century life. But as his world begins to unravel, these ancient laws start to take on new meaning.

---

1. https://books2read.com/u/me5Xnz

2. https://books2read.com/u/me5Xnz

Follow Clyde's raw, unflinching journey as he grapples with each commandment, facing the darkest parts of himself and the society around him.

This gripping tale doesn't shy away from the gritty realities of modern life. It delves deep into the human psyche, exposing the universal struggles we all face in a world that often seems to have lost its moral compass.

But "Yahweh and Clyde" is more than just a story of one man's failings. It's a powerful testament to the transformative power of faith, the enduring relevance of timeless wisdom, and the life-changing impact of divine grace.

As Clyde claws his way from the brink of self-destruction to a life of purpose and redemption, readers will find themselves questioning their own choices, reconsidering their values, and perhaps discovering a path to their own salvation.

Part gritty confessional, part spiritual awakening, "Yahweh and Clyde" is a must-read for anyone who's ever felt lost in today's chaotic world. It's a reminder that no matter how far we've strayed, the way back home is marked by signposts as old as time itself.

Prepare to be challenged, inspired, and ultimately transformed by this unforgettable journey through the Ten Commandments in the 21st century.

9 798822 768221